# EVERYTH

## - that makes ...,

# PAPA

## SPECIAL

what I Love About You...

# ~ Contents ~

1. Gratitude
2. Love
3. Fun
4. Letter to Papa

Written By...

_____

THANK YOU,
PAPA!

# 1.
# Gratitude

## Three reasons I'm GRATEFUL for you...

1. _____

2. _____

3. _____

PAPA, THANK YOU for TEACHING me how to...

_____

Thank you for ALWAYS...

_____

and helping me...

. . . . . . . . . . . . . . . . . . . . . . . . . . . . . . . .

THANK YOU for giving me...

_____

and PLAYING...

. . . . . . . . . . . . . . . . . . . . . . . . . . . . .

with me.

My FAVORITE thing to do with you is...

_____

Your hugs ALWAYS...

_____

You make me LAUGH when you...

_____

You're SPECIAL to me because...

_____

Papa, you are...

_____

(one word to describe Papa)

# Three things you're REALLY good at...

1. _____

2. _____

3. _____

Papa, you have the very BEST...

when we are together I feel...

_____

I have SO much FUN when we...

_____

together.

I know you **LOVE** me when you...

_____

My favorite memory with you was the time we...

_____

_____

because...

· · · · · · · · · · · · · · · · · · · · · · · · · · · · · · · ·

Papa, I feel SAFE when you...

_____

3.
Fun

You're stronger than...

_____

PAPA, if you could be ANY animal you would be...

_____

because...

. . . . . . . . . . . . . . . . . . . . . . . . . . . . . . . . . . . .

# Draw Papa as the animal...

I love EATING...

_____

with you.

# ~ coupons for Papa ~

Mark the box after using each coupon!

Five GIANT Hugs

Get ICE CREAM Together!

# ~ coupons for Papa ~

Mark the box after using each coupon!

## Go To The PARK
### Together!

~ Make your own coupon for Papa! ~

# 4. Letter to PAPA

~ Finish the book by writing a short letter to Papa ~

To Papa...

_____

_____

_____

_____

_____

Love From
_____

Printed in Great Britain
by Amazon

34573983R00024